A Meerkat Diary

My Journey into the Wild World
of a Meerkat Mob

This book is dedicated to Tim Farrell. Thank you for your friendship and for always supporting my work —S.E.

Owlkids Books acknowledges the financial support of the Canada Council for the Arts, the Ontario Arts Council, the Government of Canada through the Canada Book Fund (CBF) and the Government of Ontario through the Ontario Creates Book Initiative for our publishing activities.

Owlkids Books gratefully acknowledges that our office in Toronto is located on the traditional territory of many nations, including the Mississaugas of the Credit, the Chippewa, the Wendat, the Anishinaabeg, and the Haudenosaunee Peoples.

Published in Canada by Owlkids Books Inc., 1 Eglinton Avenue East, Toronto, ON M4P 3A1
Published in the US by Owlkids Books Inc., 1700 Fourth Street, Berkeley, CA 94710

Library of Congress Control Number: 2023949124

Library and Archives Canada Cataloguing in Publication
Title: A meerkat diary : my journey into the wild world of a meerkat mob / Suzi Eszterhas.
Names: Eszterhas, Suzi, author, photographer.
Identifiers: Canadiana (print) 20230580645 | Canadiana (ebook) 20230580653
 | ISBN 9781771476386 (hardcover) | ISBN 9781771477000 (EPUB)
Subjects: LCSH: Meerkat—Juvenile literature. | LCSH: Meerkat—Life
 cycles—Juvenile literature. | LCSH: Meerkat—Pictorial works—Juvenile
 literature. | LCGFT: Informational works. | LCGFT: Illustrated works.
Classification: LCC QL737.C235 E89 2024 | DDC j599.74/2—dc23

Edited by Stacey Roderick | Designed by Alisa Baldwin

MIX
Paper | Supporting responsible forestry
FSC® C010256
www.fsc.org

Manufactured in Shenzhen, Guangdong, China,
in April 2024, by WKT Co. Ltd.
Job #23CB2125

hc   A   B   C   D   E   F

ONTARIO ARTS COUNCIL
CONSEIL DES ARTS DE L'ONTARIO
an Ontario government agency
un organisme du gouvernement de l'Ontario

Canada Council
for the Arts
Conseil des arts
du Canada

Canadä

Ontario

Publisher of Chirp, Chickadee and OWL
www.owlkidsbooks.com

Owlkids Books is a division of    bayard canada

A MEERKAT DIARY

My Journey into the Wild World of a Meerkat Mob

Suzi Eszterhas

Owlkids Books

Hi! My name is Suzi Eszterhas, and I am a wildlife photographer who specializes in taking pictures of animals and their young.

My photos of big animals, such as lions, whales, gorillas, and bears, get a lot of attention, but sometimes the stories behind the pictures of the small animals are the most interesting. Meerkats, for example, are little animals with huge personalities!

I've always loved meerkats, but I knew it would be tricky to photograph them. They can be shy around people, which makes getting close to them with a camera a challenge.

Meerkats are found in only a few places in Africa, so my plan was to go to a tiny area in the heart of the Kalahari Desert in Botswana. And since meerkats can have several litters each year, it wasn't long before I found out about a mob with some newborn pups. I called my assistant, Becky, and we packed up and headed to southern Africa!

I was glad Becky could come along on this adventure. She's a zoologist, which means she has studied all kinds of animals, including meerkats. Her knowledge and experience are different from mine, so we make a great team. And we always have fun together.

This is my diary of those exciting few weeks with the meerkats.

The
Makgadikgadi
Pan

BOTSWANA

The Makgadikgadi Pan is in the Kalahari Desert in northeastern Botswana. This flat area covered in salt is all that is left of a lake that dried up tens of thousands of years ago. Meerkats live on the outer edges of the pan, as well as in deserts and grasslands in some areas of the surrounding countries.

FEBRUARY 2

It was a long trip, but we're finally here!

Sitting next to the pilot in our little bush plane, I could see the Makgadikgadi Pan ahead of us as we flew in. This area of flat land is huge—as big as the country of Switzerland! Suddenly the sunlight got so bright I could barely open my eyes. The pilot explained that all the salt left over from the dried-up lake was reflecting the sun. A little later, we landed on a tiny strip of dirt in the middle of the desert.

We drove to camp with all our gear. Motto and Villa were there waiting to meet us. Motto is a meerkat habituator, which might just be the coolest job in the world. He spends hours every day hanging around the meerkats so they become comfortable around people instead of fearful. This gives visitors a very special opportunity to observe meerkats in their natural habitat. Villa is a naturalist guide who knows everything about the desert environment. He showed us some beautiful photos he'd taken of the meerkats we'll be meeting tomorrow morning. I'm so excited, I'm not sure I'll be able to sleep tonight!

Meet the meerkat team! From left to right: Motto Keitumetse, me, Becky Cliffe, and Villa Moatshe.

Becky and I are staying in a beautiful place called Jack's Camp. We'll be sleeping in a gorgeous tent under palm trees. We feel so fortunate and grateful to be here.

FEBRUARY 3

Today we met our meerkat mob! (It always seems funny to call such cute little animals a mob, but that's the word for a meerkat community.)

Before dawn, Motto and Villa drove us to the meerkats' location. We quietly approached a large hole in the ground. This was the burrow where the meerkats live. We lay down in the grass on our bellies so we looked small and not scary to the meerkats.

Meerkat mobs have a female leader called a matriarch. This mob's matriarch, Maghogho, was the first to appear. She stuck her head out and looked around. Then she came all the way out and stood up on her hind legs. Villa explained that it gets very cold underground all night, so Maghogho was warming up by exposing her nearly bare belly to the heat of the morning sun. Standing on her back legs is also how she looks out for predators, such as birds of prey or jackals.

Motto has been doing a great job of habituating the meerkats, because even though Maghogho saw us, she wasn't afraid. Instead she made some chirping sounds—she was letting her family know it was safe to come out!

Becky and I had seen Maghogho in some documentary shows, so we recognized her right away. She must be one of the most famous meerkats in the world!

Soon a large face peeked out of the hole. The father of the pups stared at us before barking and running out to join Maghogho. He stood up to warm himself, too, but he kept a watchful eye on us. We decided to name him Stinky because he kept giving us the stink eye. Stinky was pretty new to the mob, so he hadn't been exposed to humans as much. But Motto reassured us that Stinky would soon grow to trust us.

Villa said that the meerkats sunbathe every sunny morning. What a lovely way to start the day—for the humans, too!

This was our first glimpse of the meerkat pups. Meerkat pups are born hairless, with their eyes and ears closed, and weighing only about 1 oz. (28 g). That's about the same as a slice of white bread. At two weeks old, their eyes are open, and they weigh about 4 oz. (113 g), which is a little less than a baseball.

A couple minutes later, a smaller face popped out from the hole. It was one of Maghogho's sons from an earlier litter. We'll think of a name for him once we learn a little more about his personality, but for now we are calling him Big Brother.

Next came five of the sweetest, tiniest faces—a litter of two-week-old pups! Becky said that the pups' vision hasn't developed enough to clearly see us, but they can sense us as large figures that are new to their environment. We stayed still and held our breath while their older brother gently coaxed them out of the hole. One by one, the pups came out and joined the rest of the family in the sun.

I lost track of time watching the family sunbathe and listening to them chirp away in meerkat chitchat. Suddenly Maghogho ran from the group to dig in the dirt for insects. Villa explained that she needed to eat to make more milk for her nursing babies. Then Stinky and Big Brother wandered off, too. Without adult protection, the pups ran back into the burrow for safety.

A few minutes later, Stinky came running back at full speed with a worm in his mouth. He had been hunting for breakfast for the pups! Soon Big Brother arrived with another worm. The pups popped out again, delighted. And hungry!

Stinky barked at us out of fear and uncertainty today. But I'm sure he'll soon realize that he does not have to be afraid of us.

Becky and I watched this fascinating feeding ritual for hours and didn't notice when Maghogho returned. But the pups immediately recognized her familiar mama meerkat chirp. They jumped all over her. Turns out, they were hungry for milk, too! As soon as Maghogho found a spot to rest, the pups began to suckle.

Our first day went by so fast. There were many feedings, and I took thousands of pictures. I'm already in love with this little meerkat family.

It was neat seeing one of my favorite things about meerkat society in action: the whole mob feeds, cares for, and protects the young pups. They must work together to survive!

FEBRUARY 4

Big Brother has a new name!

The meerkats spent the morning basking in the sun. We did, too! The mornings are chilly in the Kalahari, and it felt nice to warm up. Then, like yesterday, Maghogho left to search for insects to eat. This time Stinky went with her, leaving Big Brother in charge of all five pups for most of the day. And he had his hands full!

The pups were very active and curious. They each wandered off in different directions at different times, so Big Brother was busy all afternoon chasing after them and herding them back. In fact, we've decided to call him Cinderella from now on because of all the hard work he was left behind to do.

Cinderella steadies himself with his tail while he looks for signs of danger. Eventually the pups will become strong enough to copy this "tripod" stance.

Cinderella also had to be on the lookout for possible danger. Sometimes, for a better view, he climbed up on a mound of earth. A few times he even stood on my backpack. Motto said that once the meerkats felt safe enough, they might even try to stand on us!

The pups tried to copy Cinderella by standing up on their hind feet, but they kept falling over! Becky said they needed to be stronger and more coordinated to have the balance. We had to laugh as they teetered and wobbled, standing for a second and then falling down. And they didn't give up; they just got back up and tried again.

Throughout the day, Cinderella also had to feed the pups. He caught a few insects, more worms, and even a couple dung beetles! We noticed that Cinderella didn't keep a single insect for himself.

The pups were full of energy, but Cinderella was a responsible and careful babysitter.

Cinderella used my backpack as a lookout post!

Now that we've spent a couple days with the meerkats, we've started to recognize their individual personalities. Before bed Becky and I came up with our names for the five pups.

Chief

Chief is the first pup to pop out of the burrow each morning. (He is also the pup who ruins every photograph by facing the wrong way. Come on, Chief!)

Beetlejuice is a mellow little pup. She earned her name when she tried to devour a beetle and ended up with a sticky mess of beetle juice stuck in her fur all day.

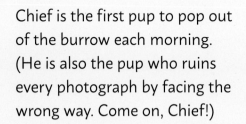

Scrammy

Scrammy bosses her siblings around. She even snapped at Cinderella several times today! She's sassy!

Runt

Runt is the smallest pup and super sweet. He moves a little slower than the others, so he usually ends up at the back of the pack when the meerkat mob moves. We hope he just needs more time to grow and catch up with his siblings.

Beetlejuice

Peeker

Peeker's shyness makes him extra cute! Each morning, all the other pups leave the burrow before him. Then when he feels ready and safe, he peeks out and cautiously makes his exit.

15

FEBRUARY 5

Today the meerkat mob had quite an adventure!

The whole family left the burrow together. Maghogho must have decided it was time to bring the pups along to explore their habitat. We could tell they were excited!

The pups followed the adults in a line, but Becky and I worried about Runt, who kept falling behind. Luckily one adult always waited for him. Villa told us that Runt was his favorite pup and not to worry because one day he would be bigger and stronger than the rest. That made me feel better.

The pups are only a few inches tall, so walking through the tall grass on their short, wobbly legs was a challenge. And all day long, they squeaked and begged for food. But the adults didn't seem bothered by the constant screeching. Becky and I decided that adult meerkats must be some of the most patient animals on Earth.

Stinky and Cinderella stayed busy finding worms, beetles, and grubs to feed the pups. And Maghogho focused on feeding herself so she could produce enough milk for the pups.

It was interesting to see how the three adults took turns at sentry duty,

Meerkats are carnivores and eat insects, spiders, scorpions, frogs, snails, rodents, eggs, lizards, and even small birds.

looking out while the others found food. Meerkats often bury their heads while digging for food, so they might not notice a nearby predator, such as a bird of prey, snake, or jackal. The sentry finds higher ground where they keep watch.

Motto explained to us that the sentry squeaks and chirps to either give the "all clear" signal or to warn the others of danger. He also taught us how to identify some of the meerkats' happy sounds. We joked that he is an expert in "speaking meerkat."

In between trips looking for food, the adults took rest breaks, with one always keeping lookout. The pups napped snuggled up in a pile of cuteness! Becky said that some researchers have special cameras to observe meerkats underground in their burrow, and meerkats sleep in a similar cuddle puddle at night.

Finally it was time to return to the burrow. We could tell the pups were exhausted from their adventure and happy to be home because they ran right down the hole and never came back out. It was their bedtime.

And now it's my bedtime, too!

We stayed extra quiet and still while the pups snoozed. We knew they needed their rest on such a busy day.

Some meerkats are better at sentry duty than others. These "super guards" stand watch twice as often as less skilled lookouts. Cinderella must be a super guard!

FEBRUARY 6

At the start of our walk to the burrow this morning, Becky and I thought we'd spotted another mob of meerkats.

As it turned out, they were actually Cape ground squirrels, which Villa found quite funny. When he stopped laughing at our mistake, he told us squirrels dig small holes that meerkats often take over and make into bigger burrows. Sometimes squirrels and meerkats will even live together in the same burrow.

On the way, we also saw an oryx munching on some grass. It was one of the most beautiful antelopes I'd ever seen! Villa told us that oryx know that grass collects dew overnight. By feeding in the early morning, they also get plenty of water before it dries up in the hot sun. So smart!

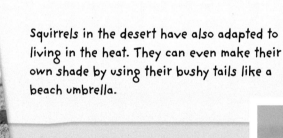

Squirrels in the desert have also adapted to living in the heat. They can even make their own shade by using their bushy tails like a beach umbrella.

This is a male oryx. Both males and females have long horns shaped like spears to protect them against predators, such as big cats and hyenas.

Yellow mongoose also sometimes share a burrow with meerkats. In fact, some very busy burrows might be home to mongoose, squirrels, and meerkats all at once.

When we arrived at the burrow, we found things were a bit different today.

We noticed the pups were moving faster and less clumsily through the sea of grass. Even Runt looked stronger and more agile!

And for the first time, Stinky didn't bark at us. In fact, he didn't pay much attention to us at all. In just a few days, he had learned to trust us!

The pups were more comfortable around us, too. Beetlejuice used my shadow as shade from the sun, while Chief, Scrammy, and Runt each tried to climb on my knee! As a wildlife photographer, I don't usually allow this. It's important that wild animals and humans keep a safe distance from one another. But the pups were determined. Thankfully, the only people these meerkats meet respect and love them.

The pups want to climb on anything they can, including us! Motto says that practicing climbing helps the pups become good sentries.

The pups run and play close to us now, so we must pay extra attention to exactly where they are. Notice we wear our pants tucked into our socks—that way nothing can crawl up our legs!

FEBRUARY 7

Meerkat sunbathing was canceled today because it was too cloudy.

But the weather didn't matter to the pups, who wanted their breakfast! Cinderella hurried out of the burrow and returned with a bunch of big dung beetles. I noticed that the pups get extra excited when he brings them food. Becky said that meerkat pups beg louder around the adults who feed them more often.

Cinderella was kept busy, bringing the pups one beetle meal after another.

Once, he brought back beetles that were still alive! At first, the pups were surprised and intimidated by the wiggling insects. But true to her name, Beetlejuice soon went in for the kill. She smacked the beetle with her little paw, grabbed it in her mouth, cracked the shell, and gulped down the messy meal!

After the beetles, Cinderella found caterpillars and other insects. In fact, the pups were so busy feasting that they stayed out of the burrow later than usual.

With five pups to feed, the meerkat adults are always busy looking for food. The adults don't feed a specific pup; they instinctively feed the pup who is closest to them when they find an insect.

As the sun went down, Stinky, who was on sentry duty, spotted the jackals on the horizon and gave his loud alarm call. Maghogho and Cinderella returned the call and raced toward the burrow, with the rest of the mob following quickly behind. Poor Runt struggled to keep up, but Stinky grabbed the pup by the scruff of his neck, just like a mother cat would carry her kitten. The mob reached their burrow and scrambled inside. Becky and I counted each pup as it went in. We were so relieved that all the pups were safe and sound. Phew!

After dinner it began to rain. It started as a light sprinkle, but it's quickly become a downpour. Lying here listening to the rain slamming onto the top of our tent, I hope the meerkats are also staying safe, warm, and dry.

Jackals and snakes are the land predators of meerkats. A meerkat is no match for a jackal and must run and hide to survive. Meerkats aren't as afraid of snakes because they can put up a good fight and may even kill a snake.

Dung beetles might be hard to crack open, but they are an excellent source of nutrition for small mammals such as meerkats.

FEBRUARY 8

Villa reported that the Makgadikgadi got one-third of its yearly rainfall in the storm last night. The entire area is flooded!

We started the drive to the meerkats, but our vehicle was soon stuck in the mud. Villa and Motto worked for hours trying to dig it out while Becky and I helped in whatever way we could. Eventually they had to call another vehicle to come get us.

We returned to camp and planned what to do next. Villa suggested walking to the meerkats, so that's what we did!

Our hiking shoes quickly filled with water. Becky and I got stuck in the deep mud a few times, and Villa and Motto had to pull us out. It was a long and challenging trek through the high water and thick mud, but we spent most of the time laughing at how ridiculous we looked! We were a mess!

When we finally made it to the meerkats, they looked like we felt—

Our vehicle couldn't get through the flooded roads, so we walked about 12.5 mi. (20 km) through thick, muddy water, carrying our heavy gear the whole way. What a workout!

wet, cold, and shivering. Miraculously the inside of their burrow looked dry. Motto explained that meerkats know to build their burrow on higher ground. That instinct helped them survive the unusual weather.

Eventually the meerkats warmed up and went off to find food.

It rained on and off all afternoon, and Becky and I struggled to keep our equipment dry. We didn't mind— both of us would gladly accept this same wet, chilly adventure again if it meant spending another day with the meerkats. Even so, I *really* hope tomorrow will be drier.

Avoiding rain on the open plains is challenging since there aren't trees or other kinds of shelter. We used our rain ponchos and tarps to protect our gear while we waited for a break in the storm.

FEBRUARY 9

Although it finally stopped raining last night, everything was still flooded when we woke up this morning. That meant we had to walk to the meerkats again, but somehow the trek seemed a little easier today.

At the burrow, it was a normal day for the meerkats until Maghogho went off in a new direction. We followed her toward lower ground, where there were pools of floodwater. Becky and I wondered why she wanted to go near the water. Meerkats dislike water and are not good swimmers.

Motto suspected that Maghogho wanted to look for insects on the other side of her territory, but she probably didn't know how deep the water was. We watched as Maghogho jumped from one island of mud and grass to the next, with her pups following close behind. At first, the pups were jumping with ease, until Chief fell in! Next, Scrammy fell in! Stinky and Cinderella were close by, along with Peeker, Beetlejuice, and Runt, but now they were all struggling in the muddy water. It was chaos!

Chief was getting tired from treading water—he was in trouble! Maghogho noticed and leaped to him, snatched him out of the water with her mouth, and carried him to a patch of dry grass. He was drenched and exhausted but out of harm's way. Next, Maghogho rescued Scrammy. Once everyone was safe, she led the mob back to higher ground, leaving the dangerous floodwater behind. Phew!

Chief struggled to stay afloat in the deep water and could have drowned. He was lucky to survive, and we were very relieved!

Maghogho strategically leaped from dry patch to dry patch, somehow managing to avoid the deep pools of water.

Many Ju/'hoansi people work with eco-tourism companies while they continue to practice important cultural traditions. Xamme showed us how he extracts water from the root of a plant. He peeled back layers of the plant's skin and then squeezed it. I was shocked to see how much water trickled out!

We headed back to camp earlier than usual today. Villa took us to meet some of the Indigenous people whose families have lived in the Makgadikgadi Pan for tens of thousands of years. The desert might look uninviting to visitors like us, but the Ju/'hoansi people are hunter-gatherers who long ago learned to adapt, survive, and thrive here. They showed us how to get water from plant roots, build fires when there is little wood available, and find delicious berries. They described how they make natural medicines and showed us some of their traditional dances. It was an incredible visit!

Over dinner later Villa told us more about the culture of the Ju/'hoansi people and the threats to their survival. They support themselves partly by hosting visiting tourists, but it's getting difficult to live their traditional way of life as more towns and farms are built around the protected areas of the Kalahari. Most of the younger people are adapting to a changing world while

One of the people we spent the afternoon with was Xoshe, who welcomed us warmly.

trying to keep parts of their history, culture, and language. The Ju/'hoansi people we met were proud of their lifestyle and generously shared some of their unique culture with us. I hope they continue to share their history and heritage with future generations so they can keep their special culture alive forever.

FEBRUARY 10

At sunrise Villa and Motto spotted a brown hyena!

Brown hyenas are mostly nocturnal, so seeing one in the daytime is rare. When we looked through our binoculars, what we saw was even more unusual—it was a mother with a tiny cub! The cub was a cute miniature version of its mother. The pair enjoyed a bit more of the morning sun, then quickly disappeared into their cool underground den to snooze the day away.

The meerkats were already out looking for food when we arrived at the burrow. We noticed the family traveled a longer distance than usual. Motto explained that the mob had probably eaten most of the insects in that location over the last few weeks, so they needed to go farther away.

Motto also wondered if the meerkats were wanting to avoid the mosquitoes that came with all the rain and puddles. That made sense because the meerkats kept stopping to paw at their faces and

Becky and I thought the brown hyena cub looked like a teddy bear! I had read about brown hyenas and had seen many pictures of them, but spotting a mother and baby in the wild was a memorable experience.

The meerkats covered a lot of distance today, and now the growing pups are managing to keep up with the adults.

shoo the annoying bugs away. And Becky and I had swarms of mosquitoes following us even though we'd lathered ourselves in repellent. It was hard to take pictures with all the buzzing and biting distractions. At one point Becky got so frustrated that she ran in circles flailing her arms while a mosquito cloud chased her. I couldn't help but laugh!

Near the end of the day, the meerkats discovered a large hole in the ground. The adults ran around investigating all parts of it. They went in and out several times,

communicating to each other with chirps and squeaks. Exhausted by the extra travel today, the pups collapsed in a heap outside the hole's entrance. Suddenly Becky and I realized that the mob would not return to the old burrow. Our meerkats had found a new home!

Weighing only 1.5 lb. (680 g) at full size, meerkats are so light that they don't always leave tracks. But in the wet mud and sand, we were able to spot the imprints from their little paws and long claws.

This morning we found the mob still tucked away in their new burrow.

I guess meerkats have lazy mornings, too! Or maybe they were enjoying their new home so much, they weren't ready to come out. Villa remembered that the meerkats had nested in this burrow before. He also said it was normal for meerkats to switch homes every few months. Apparently some meerkat burrows are huge, with up to 15 entrance and exit holes, lots of tunnels, and special areas for going to the toilet and sleeping.

When the mob finally set off to find food, the pups were extra playful. They pawed, tackled, wrestled, and nibbled on one another. We watched the playing turn into fighting when a delicious treat was around. These kinds of squabbles actually help prepare pups for adult life, when they will need to fight other meerkats for territory.

Scorpions are a favorite food of meerkats, especially Scrammy. We saw her try to steal one that Cinderella was feeding to Peeker. When she failed, Scrammy threw a frustrated tantrum. Cinderella remained patient and tried

Playing is fun and important! The pups play to build muscles and coordination, develop social skills, and learn to defend themselves.

Meerkat burrows are made up of tunnels and spaces called chambers, some as deep as 6.5 ft. (2 m) underground. The deeper parts stay dry and comfortable, no matter what the weather's like outside.

to get away, but not before naughty Scrammy bit him on the tail!

Because scorpions have stingers with venom, the adults kill them for the young pups. Then when the pups get older, the adults will bring them live scorpions, making sure to remove the stingers first. This is how the young meerkats safely learn to capture and kill scorpions. Eventually the pups will learn how to kill and eat a scorpion *with* a stinger. Becky told me that meerkats develop protection against scorpion stings over time, but this early learning process helps them hunt carefully.

It was a day of learning and not just for the meerkat pups. Every day we learn so much about these incredible creatures!

All scorpions have a painful sting, but some types are more dangerous and deadly.

It was windy today, so the pups kept close to me to avoid getting blown away. It was very cute, but they were a little *too* close to get great photos.

FEBRUARY 12

The meerkats had a big scare today! And I discovered just how well-prepared and skilled at escaping danger they are.

While the mob was out looking for food, Stinky's high-pitched bark alerted them to danger. The entire family panicked and ran into a nearby hole. We could hear them chattering nervously inside. Becky and I looked around for jackals or other predators but didn't see any.

After some time the meerkats slowly emerged from the hole and stared up at the sky. That's when we realized there was an eagle circling the area. I could barely see it, but the adult meerkats watched it intently. Villa told me meerkats have incredible eyesight and can see objects or predators more than half a mile (one kilometer) away.

Motto also explained that meerkats have a specific sound to warn of land predators (such as jackals) and another for air predators (such as hawks and eagles). They dig emergency holes, called bolt holes, all over their territory. Then, when they hear the alarm, they run for the nearest bolt hole. I was surprised to learn that these holes are often bigger than burrows. Motto has seen a mob of 50 meerkats in a bolt hole at one time!

Meerkats have incredible eyesight and can see great distances. They can even look directly into the sun. The dark fur around their eyes acts like built-in sunglasses.

After a long time, the meerkats calmed down and communicated with quieter calls to show they were no longer on high alert. Once the eagle threat was gone, the meerkats quickly returned to searching for insects for the rest of the day. The day's excitement seemed to be over. Or that's what I thought.

As we made our way back to our tent after dinner, I gasped when I saw what was on the path—a porcupine! He was a bit shy, especially since we had been talking loudly before we spotted him. Somehow I managed to get a pretty good photo anyway.

Even though I've been all over the world as a nature photographer, Makgadikgadi has so many animals I'm seeing for the first time in my life!

The mob can watch eagles from the safety of the bolt hole. Meerkats memorize the locations of bolt holes in their territory so they can run to the closest one at a moment's notice.

Cape porcupines are the largest porcupines in the world. When in danger, they bristle their razor-sharp quills, rattle their tails, stomp their feet, hiss, and even snort. If the attacker isn't scared away, the porcupines whip around and charge backward or sideways to stab the predator with their quills.

Meerkats share their habitat with fork-tailed drongos, who can be very sneaky. They can actually fool meerkats by mimicking their alarm sounds. Why would they do that? The sounds trick the meerkats into running to their bolt holes and abandoning their food, giving drongos the opportunity to steal it.

I still can't believe what happened today even as I'm writing about it.

We were lying flat on our bellies watching the meerkats when we heard a quiet rumbling. We looked up to see a herd of zebras on the horizon. They were far away, or so we thought, until the ground started to shake. The noise got louder, and we realized the zebras were running straight toward us!

The meerkats perked their heads up to watch the massive herd of moving stripes. The adults sounded their alarm calls, and the mob ran into the nearest bolt hole. Becky said she wished we had a hole that was big enough to dive into.

I laughed nervously but secretly wished for one, too. My heart was beating fast.

But Villa told us to stay right where we were in the grass and reassured us that we would be fine. I trusted him, but I was still scared. Then he and Motto bravely stood up to show the zebras we were in their path! The zebras responded by fanning out and galloping right around us. The ground shook, the wind swirled, and we held our breath as they sprinted past us. Luckily for us they instinctively avoid things in their path when fleeing. Wow! What an incredible experience!

Nap time! Snuggled up in the safety of their bolt hole, the mob fell asleep.

Every year during the rainy season, zebras migrate to the Makgadikgadi area to feed on lush new grass. Between 25,000 and 30,000 zebras share the tasty grass!

After the dust settled and our hearts stopped pounding, we wondered what had scared the zebras in the first place. Villa scanned the area for lions with his binoculars but didn't see any. Becky said that zebras often travel together in big herds, and sometimes one zebra might accidentally spook the others and cause a full-on stampede.

When the meerkats eventually came out of their bolt hole, it was bath time! The adults used their teeth to carefully remove insects and dirt from each other's fur. Then they cleaned the pups, who haven't learned to groom yet. Social grooming keeps meerkats healthy and strengthens their family bonds. It's almost as meaningful as snuggling. And just as cute!

On our way back to camp later, we had another wild animal sighting— and this time it was a lion! It was a male Kalahari lion with a beautiful dark mane. Villa said that Kalahari lions are smaller than lions in other regions. But even from far away, he still looked massive to me.

After this encounter we couldn't help but wonder … was it the lion that spooked the zebras?

Lions have learned to survive in the desert, too. For example, they lick dewdrops off grass when water is scarce.

Clean fur is important for the health of a meerkat. Each adult in the mob participates in social grooming to remove ticks, fleas, ants, and other pests.

FEBRUARY 14

Becky and I woke up feeling sad today. It was our last day with the meerkats!

The meerkats were busy with housekeeping chores in the morning. Motto explained that dirt and sand sometimes shift inside the burrow. The mob tidies it up from time to time—otherwise their home could cave in and bury them!

We watched the adults dig around the burrow. Meerkats have special adaptations that make them some of the best diggers on the planet. First, they have long, powerful claws. Second, they have a clear membrane that covers and protects their eyes from flying sand. Third, they have ears that can fold shut so dirt doesn't get in.

Though the pups also tried to dig, they weren't very good at it. They soon gave up and played around and practiced the tripod stance instead. The meerkat pups can stand on their hind legs longer now. And Runt has had a growth spurt! He is nearly the same size as his siblings, and he looks stronger and healthier than before. Villa said, "I told you! He will be just fine."

The rest of the day was filled with scorpion chasing, nap time, lots of play … until an amazing thing happened!

Meerkats don't need shovels. Their long claws are excellent digging tools.

Becky was crouching near her video equipment when Maghogho ran up from behind and climbed her back to look out over the plains. Becky froze with surprise. Well, of course the pups were curious, and one by one, they joined mom on Becky's back! Then they made themselves even *more* comfortable up there and started to suckle! I had to laugh at this odd situation. Becky didn't know what to do, so she just let them hang out there for a while.

What a funny end to our amazing adventure! For almost two weeks, we followed these adorable little beings from sunrise to sunset—and they had welcomed us into their mob. We fell in love with each of them. It was an incredible experience to watch the pups grow and learn how to hunt scorpions and protect themselves from danger. We plan to return and reunite with these pups when they are all grown up. Until then we will root for them to survive and thrive!

Becky stayed still when Maghogho and the pups were on her back. She didn't want to frighten them with any small or sudden movements. It was hard for both of us not to laugh!

Digging is hard work. Cinderella spent lots of time clearing an exit hole in the burrow.

MEET MOTTO AND VILLA

Motto and Villa are an incredible team. They taught us so much, but we also wanted to learn a bit more about them. Here are some of the questions we asked them while we were together:

Motto, how did you become a meerkat habituator?

I grew up in a local village not far from here called Gweta and always loved animals as a little boy. Eight years ago I was lucky enough to be offered this job. I learned how to habituate meerkats by working with the more experienced staff members, who taught me everything I know.

What is the hardest part about your job?

This job requires a lot of patience. When I am following a new mob, they run from me for the first two or three months, so I have to stay very far away. It takes a whole year to fully habituate a mob.

What is your favorite part of your job?

Meerkats are always doing something exciting. They are very social and always interacting with each other. They can be kind one minute and absolutely vicious the next. They are never boring!

Motto

Villa

Villa, what is your favorite animal in the Kalahari?

It is very difficult to pick just one. I used to work at a rhino sanctuary and fell in love with rhinos. And then for the first three years working here, I was absolutely fascinated by meerkats. But recently I've become drawn to African wildcats. They are the closest relative of house cats and remind me of one I had growing up. His name was Mmampokosa, and I loved him very much.

Did you always want to work with animals?

No, I actually used to want to be an accountant. It was considered a good, stable job to have. But then I figured out that wildlife and conservation are my greatest passions. I decided to follow my dreams, and I am so glad I did.

Why did you choose to become a naturalist guide?

I decided to study guiding because it is a great way to educate tourists about the threats to wildlife and what they can do to help them. Part of my job is also to talk to local people to teach them how to coexist with wild animals that live in or near their communities.

THE WILDLIFE CONSERVATION NETWORK (WCN)

For over 20 years, WCN has helped conservationists protect endangered wildlife in Africa and throughout the world. They have raised hundreds of millions of dollars for wildlife conservation efforts and supported hundreds of projects that protect specific threatened species—such as elephants, lions, rhinos, and pangolins. WCN also invests in local conservationists by offering scholarships and grants in order to strengthen their skills, advance their careers, and continue to build their organizations. Suzi is donating a large portion of the proceeds from this book to WCN.

Words to Know

burrow: the underground home of an animal

hunter-gatherer: a traditional way of living on a diet of hunted animals and gathered plants

Indigenous people: the first people that lived in an area and their descendants

matriarch: a female leader of a family or social group

meerkat habituator: a skilled person who helps meerkats become less fearful of humans

mob: a group of meerkats that live together

naturalist guide: a local wildlife and nature expert who educates visitors and local people

nocturnal: an animal that is most active at night

predator: an animal that hunts and eats other animals

salt pan: a large, flat area of land covered in salt left behind by a dried-out body of salt water

sentry: a guard

suckle: the way a young mammal feeds on its mother's milk by sucking

territory: an area that an animal marks and protects as its own

venom: a poisonous liquid that an animal uses, usually by biting or stinging, to protect itself